THE TEMPLE

THE TEMPLE

POEMS

MICHAEL BAZZETT

BULL★CITY
PRESS

DURHAM, NORTH CAROLINA

The Temple

Editors' Selection from the 2020 Frost Place Chapbook Competition

Library of Congress Cataloging-in-Publication Data
Bazzett, Michael
The Temple: poems / by Michael Bazzett
p.   cm.
ISBN-13: 978-1-949344-16-5

Published in the United States of America

Book design by Spock and Associates

"Silhouette" photo by Steven Roberge
Licensed under https://creativecommons.org/licenses/by/2.0/

Published by
BULL CITY PRESS
1217 Odyssey Drive
Durham, NC 27713

www.BullCityPress.com

CONTENTS

for Leslie

If you find you no longer believe, enlarge the temple.

—W. S. Merwin

THE END

In the beginning, God wanted
to be a comedian. *What is made
in my image, but has no soul?*
he'd ask, and just stare at you,
exchanging the idea of a punch
line for something like endless
exhalation. He would raise
one eyebrow and ash his cigar.
No laughter. Part of the issue
was the slight skew in the angels'
sense of humor. Sometimes
dozens would sit and watch
the obstinate waves batter a
glacier for weeks, only laughing
when it calved and a shattered
hunk of dirty ice lunged free
into the frigid Antarctic sea.
Then they'd bray like donkeys.
God took notes and tried using
a similar structure: the build
that starts to feel like boredom.
Good timing's probably tough
when you're eternal. Jokes,
like most folks, have no idea
what they mean until the end.

THE ONES WHO AREN'T MENTIONED

I like the stories best about the ones who aren't
mentioned.
          The offhand reference to the ears
of the serial killer's dog, relaxing back
          when her master enters the room, how
                    her tail steadily *thunks* the carpet.

    Or maybe the mouse watching the city burn,
flames twitching in the dark beads of her eyes.

She scutters later among the cinders, worried
about falcons, worried about hawks, her quick tongue
testing the stains beneath each body, for salt.
                    I can almost see her now,
    clutching a single seed in her tiny pink hands.

                There are entire religions that tell
of a God who refused to say who he was:
child, man, ghost?
          Or maybe even a luminous mist
that hovered in the dark before dawn kissed
the windowsill with light?
                    Imagine watching a son
die and saying nothing. Imagine laying down

a rusty knife and calling it love.

SOMETIMES THE BODY GETS TIRED

of filtering everything.

      Alcohol and cigarettes, of course. But also
rage.
             My kidneys are currently
filthy with grief. There is a quiet sadness that often
settles over me a few hours after my coffee.
                     Death
seems almost a happiness to the man with one foot

nailed to the floor and a ravenous wolf at his door.
Watching your children grow finely strong
                    as the pouches
beneath your eyes collapse into wrinkled wineskins
is a special form of yoga.
           One part of you stretches
up toward sky, thin as smoke, while the other
roots down solid in the earth, chomping like a worm.

THE TUNNEL

I entered the tunnel—crumbling brick, smell of moss—
and walked toward the pinprick of light.

It was so dark I held my hand before me, high-stepping
over the uneven stones, hearing water plink

and seep among the scuttle of small animals. The man
in the iron–gray uniform looked startled

when I emerged. Where'd you come from? he said.
The other end, I replied. But this is the main entrance,

he said, pointing up to the iron sign
weeping stains of rust down the façade: AMNESIA $100

A crowd of silent people stood waiting for admittance,
huddled under umbrellas behind a thin brass chain.

But I didn't know, I said, patting my pockets for a ticket
that wasn't there. No worries, said the man.

Coming in from that way only costs a buck. I dug out
a single crumpled dollar and handed it to him. Be careful,

he smirked as he pocketed the bill. They say
if you only walk it backwards, you end up with nostalgia.

I HAD A LITTLE TROUBLE BELIEVING IN GOD

but the empty grave was no problem.

Belief in the honed bronze spear-tip
releasing the gush
of water followed by the thick blood
that hurried his expiration
as he hung wasted on the cross

was also easy.

I could almost see the bored centurions
craving a drink
as the shadows crept in.

And the sour tang of vinegar
they thrust at him,
the sponged wine on a stick?

Easy. Just put lemon on sun-cracked lips
and close your eyes. Imagine nails
thick as crude spikes. Feel it burn.

But the holes are what I remember
best. How you could see
a tiny glimmer of sunlight
in the center of his palm

whenever he raised a hand
to wave goodbye.

THE REASONABLY GOOD SHEPHERD

after Vasko Popa

guards the stones
scattered across the meadow.

It's better this way, he said.

I don't have to worry
about them wandering.

Wolves leave them alone.

And from a distance, they
still dot the field with white.

But what do you do for wool,
milk, cheese?

Oh, I milk them, he said

and the milk is thick
and cures everything

but loneliness.

He stood to leave and seemed
as surprised as we were

when his herd began
to follow him

with a sound
like distant thunder.

THE TEMPLE

I am considering building an addition
to my temple. Perhaps
something modern. For instance, a transparent
box of glass erupting from the walls
of rough-cut stone
as if an aquarium were making
love to a monastery.

This would give me
a place to take my tea in the morning light
that would perhaps be less drafty
than the rest of the temple

which has haunting archways
and sonorous acoustics
but can be a little damp.

Also, I think I need a little more
space for my imagination
which sometimes sighs like a tired dog
after half a hundred years.

Those would be my years,
not dog-years. Because that dog
would be roughly three hundred
and forty-something and this attempt

at sincerity would become patently
unbelievable and ultimately
what we are talking about here

is belief. And I want the temple
to hold more not less.
I will say to the architects:

Make my temple beautiful
the way it was when I was a boy
and thought that God,
even if he did not actually live there,
might occasionally wander in
to check out the acoustics

and maybe lift his voice
in a song of praise
to something other than himself—

OUR BODIES

We used to ditch them after school,

dropping them in the lush grass
that grew where the trestle bridge
crossed the creek and everything
smelled of fish and tarred timber.

Then we sank to the silty bottom
of the stream and stared up
through the rusty water for hours

without worrying about breathing,

and when trains rumbled overhead
raining gravel and cinders down
into the creek, we did not blink.

Afterward we crept back to where
our bodies lay tangled in the grass,
still as two steamed fish on a plate,

and we peered into our empty eyes

then climbed back into our skins
and felt heavy at first and too thick,

and sometimes you would even cry
a little on the way home and when
I'd try to comfort you, you'd say,

No its okay, sometimes it just hits
me this way, living inside a body.

THE EMPTY CITY

I went to the doctor and found out
there is an empty city inside me.

The streets are broad and mostly clean.
Trees are few and far between.
No cars are parked on the boulevards.

Why has it been abandoned, this city?
Who used to live here, and why
did they rush off to the countryside?

I admit I was distressed by the news.
I had hoped for a mist-cloaked wilderness,
or at least a ragged branch of crows.

Instead I wander silent apartments.
The closets brim with winter clothes.

Now I lie awake and wonder: what will they
do when the winds of November come
and bite through their thin summer dresses?

TELL ME AGAIN

after Robert Bly

Tell me about the sound of wind in the pines,
the cushioned duff, the needles that make
a clean floor and bring a hush to the understory.

Tell me how deer come here at night
to curl into ovals, how they dream of windfall
apples, a scent like wine, how when they dream
of wolves, their hooves kick out like knives.

I can see the tamped outlines of their beds,
where they scuffle into needles that cling to them
like fine red parentheses. Tell me how at nightfall,

I split in two and the other half of me comes here
to these trunks, where I lie among the deer, and the sides
of our bodies barely touch with every rising breath.

GOD

for Ada Límon

Look, it's not that I believe in him. Nor he
in me. We have moved beyond all that.
I just like having someone there in the dark.
Usually we sit in silence, waiting for passing
headlights to glide across the ceiling and knock
stray prayers loose from where they got
stuck on their way out, so many years ago.
It's almost like finding old piñata candy,
says God, picking one from the floorboards.
He unwraps it, takes a quick taste. Winces.
Nods like he's just remembered something
for the thousandth, thousandth time.
What is it? I ask. It's kind of like chewing
tinfoil, he says. All that aching naked hope.

I ENTER INTO THE COLD

and walk to the lake and then out across it,
looking for something to bless: maybe a hole
grown closed after the ice-fisherman left
and dragged his auger home on a sledge,
maybe the smattering of silver minnows
he cast aside, wide-eyed, frozen hard as glass,
maybe the hard afternoon light scraping
low across the scalded crusts of snow, maybe
something, anything that I could offer here
that would make us feel there is a marvelous
truth in looking
                        but my dog is not looking
and finds instead the space unexpectedly
open and calling to him and he runs and he
bounds huge circles into this temporary
vastness on spring-coiled legs that are also
temporary, and with every passing minute
the engines of his body incinerate roughly
seven minutes of mine and the heat this
makes rises in white huffs from his lungs
and I stop looking to bless to be blessed
to do anything but listen to my animal
burn the air into a kind of living smoke—

A CONFESSION

When my dog started rewriting my poems,
they got better. They suddenly possessed
the ineffable whiff of multivalent scents
milked from the breeze by a wet black nose,
the ear-flopping joy of open car windows,
the quivering willingness to lick the ones
you barely know but sense that you might
one day love. The squirrel imagery grew
more pungent, more *necessary*, the piercing
musk of unbathed human flesh rose sharp
as wine intermingled with uncured salami,
and when the pages closed at last, you only
had to follow the circle of your own steps
before collapsing into an untroubled sleep.

REMEMBER?

Remember when we found ourselves

in that strange little gallery?
Where every painting was by a different painter and every portrait
was of you?

The Alice Neel was lovely: the almost
over-attention to detail in your face easily conveyed the intensity
of your inner life,

while the lightly sketched limbs said everything
that needed to be said of how you don't fully live in this world.

I was also fond of the brushstrokes in the Ernst Kirchner, how
they felt like thumbprints on my forehead as I looked at them.

But there could be no doubt as to my favorite.

It was the Hieronymus Bosch
where you were delicately lifting the hem of your shirt
which was also somehow the upper lip of a giant fish
and the teeth lining your stomach
were about to devour a tiny medieval cathedral
which was in the midst of being invaded
by men with the heads of frogs.

It was just so—I don't know—*you*.

CAIN & ABEL, REVISITED

So the first death on earth was murder.
And it was God who spurred it. Pitting
one against the other, then proclaiming
he preferred the smell of meat crackling
and spattering on the fire. Wood-smoke
won out over eggplant. Huge shock, that.

We all have to make sacrifices, muttered
God when I showed him my initial draft.
Then he let the paper fall to the tablecloth
and looked out the window at the snow
dropping slow as tired hands in the dusk.

He poured a little more cognac and said
he'd probably do some things differently
given the chance. His dog approached
the table then and thrust her bearded chin
firm against God's thigh, wagging her tail
as his hand cupped her head and began
to slowly knead the skin behind her ears.

She closed her eyes and God relaxed a bit.
Best thing I ever did, he said, was to make
this skull fit so snug within a human hand.

THE DEAD WOMAN

Her teeth were blue. Not bright
blue by any stretch. More like
she'd been eating blueberries
and her teeth had gotten stained,
perhaps because her enamel
had been rendered more porous
due to the lemon curd, and then
a team of experts had arrived,
removing their jackets and rolling
up their sleeves to use their tiny
brushes to scrub her teeth
with some kind of gritty paste,
yet that blue tint had nonetheless
hung on. Yes. It was more like
something white remembering
the idea of blue than blue
itself. Other than that, she was
perfectly normal. Her slightly
heathered sweater, her jeans,
the way her hair fell across her
eyes and needed to be tucked
in tendrils behind her ears, but
then she'd smile and a slight
chill would fall across the room.
This is how we knew she had
already died at least once. Maybe

twice. Yet she had no idea. She
would hold her wine and toss
her hair and smile and say, "Maybe
I'll call my next book *The Bible*
so I know my mother will read it!"
And we would laugh jovially
while still feeling a slight whinge
somewhere in our bodies, a place
near the liver, under organs
we could not possibly name.

Yet occasionally, if the night
was cold and wine emptied easily
from the bottle as we tore rough
hunks from the baguette, she'd say
things that made us wonder, like,
"Sometimes I just get so sick
of all this *stuff,* you know? I walk
into a store to buy deodorant
and eighty dollars later I'm holding
all this *stuff* made by children
in Malaysia or Guatemala
and I think, What is the point?"

Or, "Yesterday, driving home
from yoga, I passed this woman
standing at a bus stop, completely

resigned, and I thought, How
long has it been since she's felt
totally *alive?* You know? Like
when is the last time someone
walked up behind her and traced
his finger along her shoulder
because he happened to think
she was beautiful?" The blue
of her teeth disappeared in these
late-night ruminations, swallowed
up by the dusky candlelight.
It was possible to think she was
just a young woman, her life
still unfurling before her while
the rest of us traded quiet glances,
knowing all her tenderness
had never really had a chance.

THE MIRACLE

I set out the bottle of *Châteauneuf-du-Pape*,
      the hunk of manchego, crusty bread,
a little dish of olive oil with crushed
      black pepper, then pour the wine
with that lovely fluting sound lilting
      out toward the armchair where he sits.
I settle in across from him, hold my glass
      to my nose, inhale, and say, "Maybe
one of your best ideas ever, my friend."
      He smiles. "Sometimes things just
happen. Like grape juice going bad.
      It's just trying to get back to the earth
it came from." He hovers one hand
      above his glass, and the color falls
away as easily as a silk scarf dropping
      to the floor. Nothing but clear water.
He lifts the glass. "It's from the well
      on your grandparents' farm, laced
with the taste of that tin cup they kept
      by the spigot. Remember?" And I do.
It holds the mossy green taste of my
      childhood. We fall silent. The wine
is good. I can even taste the hints
      of leather mentioned on the little card
at the store, where it was proclaimed
      earthy, "brooding," and a little fierce.

But I mostly just want a drink from
        that well. "How long have you been
turning wine into water?" I ask,
        striving for an airy tone that ends
up sounding peeved. "Isn't the opposite
        more your thing?" "If you recall,
that was actually a favor for my mom,"
        he shrugs. "I guess you could say
that was more of a young man's miracle."
        He keeps talking, but I'm not
even paying attention anymore, because outside
        the meadow has grown thick
with butterflies, and the air is littered with wings.

MY BODY TELLS ME WHAT TO DO

There is still a meaty part of me
that yearns to rest
in dirt and grow soft as a mashed root.
Yet more and more,
I read of ash. How the future is made
of cinders. I am currently doing what I can
to resist pointing out
that all this earning and yearning moves
inexorably toward burning and the urn, but that weird ear-song
clearly held too much music
for me not to say it here. Or to want to hear you
murmur it too. In the incremental stew
of the *souterrain*, we settle
into ourselves so profoundly we disappear.
First, dirt
then root then pollen and wing then
aloft into nothingness. Every burial becomes
a sky burial, if you wait.
We surface. Even the low and tender
grass kisses air.
Of all the people born on earth,
only a thin fraction are alive now. So today and every day
is international ghost day.
When the dirt whispers,
it is merely your mother
calling in the gray light of dawn, tugging you

out from the soft but insistent hands of a dream
that holds you in the same way
that light is held by the icicle.

#1 HIT SONG

It's time to write a hit song, and God is not happy.
Why the loops? Why the endless repetition? he says,
slamming the headphones down on the console.
The producer stares off into space. It's not science,
he says after a moment, but there are formulas.
God opens the door to the alleyway and releases
a smattering of applause. It is actually the sound
of rain. When he returns, his hair is damp and he
smells of cigarettes. Look, he says, conciliatory,
this isn't exactly working. Would it be possible
to darken the lights while I just sit at the piano?
The producer nods. Somebody lights a candle.
God slips onto the stool, tugs gently at his beard,
frames a few hesitant minor chords then lifts his
voice into a haunting falsetto that is unbelievably
bad. It sounds like cat sex, like someone hurting
a child. But God's so damn happy, no one cares.

THE FOLLOWER

Descending the stone staircase that connects the two avenues
I saw the familiar

curve of his bald head below—
what little hair he had was cropped, so the shape was unmistakable,

as was the blue wool sweater,
though with its shiny elbows it was clearly more

worn than the one in my closet.
Running across him like this was so utterly unexpected, so

arresting that I began to follow at what I deemed a safe distance,
neglecting the grocery list

folded into one of my pockets:
almonds, lamb chops, olive oil, red peppers, basmati rice, basil,

all the food that had made the man walking in front of me
precisely what he was:

an older version of me, walking in the street, many years from now.
The scarf from my children

was wrapped around his neck, faded almost beyond recognition,
but I was glad to see he'd finally

gotten himself some well-made shoes.
I can't tell you the questions that passed through my mind, questions

he'd already pondered on this strange morning years ago
and long since forgotten.

I contemplated proposing coffee, wondered who would be more nervous,
but he seemed in something of a hurry,

and I couldn't read his expression when he stopped at the intersection:
preoccupied, tired, simply anxious

about the hour, or could that be
a look of contentedness, with a trace of something like

acceptance for the past that was following behind him even now,
a grocery list in its pocket,

taking pleasure in his undiminished stride,
which steadily receded as I stopped to watch him disappear.

ACKNOWLEDGMENTS

Thank you to the editors of the following journals, in which many of these poems first appeared.

32 poems: "God," "The Miracle"

The Adroit Journal: "The Reasonably Good Shepherd"

American Poetry Review: "The End," "Cain & Abel, Revisited"

Beloit Poetry Journal: "Our Bodies," "Tell Me Again"

Cincinnati Review: "Remember?"

diode: "My Body Tells Me What to Do," "The Follower"

Guernica: "The Dead Woman," "The Empty City"

Image: "I Had a Little Trouble Believing in God"

Poetry Northwest: "The Temple"

Prairie Schooner: "Sometimes the Body Gets Tired"

The Sewanee Review: "The Ones Who Aren't Mentioned"

West Branch: "The Tunnel"

My deep appreciation goes out to the friends, editors and mentors who read these poems in earlier incarnations and made them better with their careful attention: Justin Boening, Anders Carlson-Wee, Melissa Crowe, George David Clark, Kwame Dawes, Jamaal May, and Devon Walker-Figueroa. Huge thanks, too, to Ross and Noah at Bull City for believing in this book and making it beautiful. Finally, deepest thanks to Leslie, Sean, and Bruno, without whom these poems would never have been written. I'm forever grateful.

ABOUT THE AUTHOR

Michael Bazzett has published three books of poems: *You Must Remember This* (Winner of the Linquist & Vennum Prize for Poetry, Milkweed, 2014), *Our Lands Are Not So Different* (Horsethief Books, 2017), and *The Interrogation* (Milkweed, 2017). His fourth collection, *The Echo Chamber*, is forthcoming from Milkweed Editions in 2021. His work has appeared in journals such as *The Sun*, *American Poetry Review*, *Image*, *Threepenny Review*, and *Ploughshares*, and his verse translation of the Mayan creation epic, *The Popol Vuh*, (Milkweed, 2018) was longlisted for ALTA's National Translation Award, as well as being named one of 2018's ten best books of poetry by *The New York Times*. He lives with his wife and children in Minneapolis. You can find out more at www.michaelbazzett.com.

ALSO BY MICHAEL BAZZETT

The Imaginary City
You Must Remember This
Our Lands Are Not So Different
The Interrogation
The Popol Vuh (translation)